WORKBOOK

Meeting the Collaboration Challenge

Developing Strategic Alliances Between Nonprofit Organizations and Businesses

The Drucker Foundation

INTRODUCTION BY James E. Austin
AND Frances Hesselbein

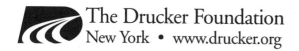
The Drucker Foundation
New York • www.drucker.org

JOSSEY-BASS
A Wiley Company
www.josseybass.com

Published by

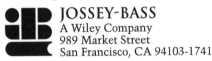

JOSSEY-BASS
A Wiley Company
989 Market Street
San Francisco, CA 94103-1741

www.josseybass.com

ISBN: 0-7879-6231-7

Printed in the United States of America

We at Jossey-Bass strive to use the most environmentally sensitive paper stocks available to us. Our publications are printed on acid-free recycled stock whenever possible, and our paper always meets or exceeds minimum GPO and EPA requirements.

FIRST EDITION

PB Printing   10 9 8 7 6 5 4 3

Contents

PHASE 1

Prepare Your Nonprofit Organization to Meet the Collaboration Challenge   1

PHASE 2

Plan Your Nonprofit Organization's Strategic Alliances with Businesses   17

PHASE 3

Develop Strategic Alliances with Businesses   29

PHASE 4

Renew Your Nonprofit Organization's Strategic Alliances with Businesses

Appendixes

Introduction:
Leading Beyond the Walls

Across the world, leaders of organizations from all three sectors increasingly recognize the necessity of *leading beyond the walls* by developing partnerships that thrive on the shared strengths of their participants. The value of productive alliances for building healthy, cohesive communities has long been clear to leaders of nonprofit social sector organizations. The challenges our society faces cannot be met—nor our opportunities fully realized—by any one organization or sector alone. Effective collaboration with other nonprofits, government agencies, and businesses is an imperative.

We are witnessing a proliferation of powerful partnerships between nonprofit organizations and businesses. The development of these strategic and complex relationships is profiled in *The Collaboration Challenge: How Nonprofits and Businesses Succeed Through Strategic Alliances* (Jossey-Bass, 2000). James Austin's book provides extensive case studies, frameworks, and lessons to help nonprofit organizations and businesses connect with each other, ensure strategic fit, generate value, and manage their relationships.

Developing effective nonprofit-business collaborations is a demanding task but quite achievable. This workbook, the accompanying thirty-minute videotape, and additional information on the Drucker Foundation Web site are designed to complement *The Collaboration Challenge* and help your nonprofit organization further its mission through strategic alliances with businesses. These resources can be used, alone or in combination, to encourage your board, volunteers, and staff to consider carefully whether and how to develop alliances with businesses. Through this systematic process for developing your nonprofit's portfolio of alliances with businesses, you can introduce concepts and examples, stimulate discussion, and unleash the creative energy of the organization.

Successful alliances justify the investment of focused attention and other resources because they directly further both the nonprofit and business missions. The thousands of practitioners who have read *The Collaboration Challenge* discovered powerful frameworks for thinking about alliances and practical guidance for designing more productive relationships. Our research, conferences, and workshops confirmed the value of this information, and our customers expressed interest in having additional practical tools to help their nonprofits develop alliances.

Inspired by *The Collaboration Challenge* and feedback from nonprofit practitioners, this workbook presents a four-phase process to help your organization *prepare* to meet the collaboration challenge, *plan* strategic alliances with businesses, *develop* alliances with businesses, and periodically *renew* business alliances. Each phase is designed to encourage appropriate participation, organize necessary information, and guide board, volunteer, and staff discussions toward successful nonprofit-business alliances.

The Drucker Foundation Vision 2010 sees the social sector as the "equal partner of business and government in developing responsible leaders, caring citizens, and a healthy, inclusive society." In this position of equity, all social sector nonprofit organizations must *lead beyond the walls* by forming partnerships, alliances, and collaborations that produce mutual benefits and results. They must be aware of the assets they possess, alert to the benefits they require, and able to act on opportunities to further their missions of building community and *changing lives*.

We look forward to learning how you have used these resources and how the Drucker Foundation may better serve social sector organizations in developing successful alliances with businesses. Please take a moment to complete and return the feedback form at the back of this workbook. We wish you the best as your organization meets the collaboration challenge to further its mission.

January 2002

James E. Austin
John G. McLean Professor of Business Administration
Chair of the HBS Initiative on Social Enterprise
Harvard Business School

Frances Hesselbein
Chairman of the Board of Governors
The Peter F. Drucker Foundation for Nonprofit Management

Acknowledgments

The board and staff of the Drucker Foundation are grateful to the collaboration partners who made this workbook (and the accompanying video) possible. We thank James E. Austin for *The Collaboration Challenge* and his long-standing devotion to the social sector and to understanding how it can grow through cross-sector alliances. For leading beyond the walls, we thank Frances Hesselbein, chairman of the Drucker Foundation Board of Governors, and long-time practitioner in building productive partnerships. This workbook is the product of many authors. Jim Austin provided the frameworks, cases, lessons, and oversight that are its thoughtful and heartfelt basis. We thank Holly Hartstone, Jill Markowitz, and Gary J. Stern, who crafted a process true to Jim Austin's work and to nonprofit practice. Sonya Grier provided a review of literature on nonprofit-business collaboration, and other members of the Drucker Foundation Training Team contributed numerous insights. The review and participation of many nonprofit leaders also contributed to the development of the workbook. We thank the hundreds of leaders at the Drucker Foundation conference and at the Peter F. Drucker School of Claremont Graduate University who reviewed the first efforts, and the members of the Milwaukee nonprofit community who reviewed the subsequent draft and workshop and provided the essential voice of the customer. For help with this Milwaukee pilot we thank Leigh Kunde of the Nonprofit Management Center for hosting, Richard Pieper of PieperPower for financial support, and the many others who assisted. We thank Ken Witty for producing the *Meeting the*

Collaboration Challenge Video. It presents real stories of collaboration success. Our publishing partners at Jossey-Bass joined us in the development and launch of these tools. We are grateful for this ongoing collaboration. Finally, we are grateful to our funders who enabled this dispersed team to collaborate.

Rob Johnston
President and CEO
Drucker Foundation

Lead Funding
> W. K. Kellogg Foundation

Additional Funding
> GE Fund
> John A. McNeice Jr.
> ServiceMaster Company
> United Way of New York City
> University of St. Thomas
> Washington Mutual
> Drucker Foundation members and funding partners

Using This Workbook and Related Resources

This workbook, its companion videotape, and the Drucker Foundation Web site are designed to complement James Austin's *The Collaboration Challenge*. Together these resources can help your nonprofit organization further its mission through strategic alliances with businesses.

These resources can be used, alone or in combination, to encourage your board, volunteers, and staff to consider carefully whether and how to develop alliances with businesses. Here are brief overviews of these resources.

The Collaboration Challenge

James Austin's book provides extensive case studies, frameworks, and lessons. It is the primary source for the Drucker Foundation's *Meeting the Collaboration Challenge* resources.

Meeting the Collaboration Challenge Workbook

This workbook provides a step-by-step process for nonprofits to explore and develop alliances with businesses. It is useful both for organizations with limited alliance experience and for organizations that have established alliances.

Nonprofit leaders can choose which phases and worksheets are most helpful to their own situation. Additional resources can help leaders explore the topics most important to their work.

Meeting the Collaboration Challenge Video

The videotape is a powerful tool that introduces examples of nonprofit business alliances and demonstrates how the ideas presented in the book and workbook are expressed in action. The video illustrates alliances' benefits and challenges as nonprofit and business leaders explain how their partnerships have developed and evolved.

Drucker Foundation Web Site [drucker.org/collaboration/]

The Web site provides this workbook in a downloadable format and presents additional current resources for meeting the collaboration challenge, including information about related workshops and how to subscribe to the monthly Meeting the Collaboration Challenge e-mail notice.

Relationships Between Nonprofit Organizations and Businesses

Process options for

BUILDING UNDERSTANDING

Your nonprofit organization's board of directors and management team may wish to build their understanding about the evolving range of relationships between nonprofits and businesses and the benefits these relationships can provide. This understanding helps the organization respond to opportunity and seek out business partners to develop alliances that further the organization's mission.

This introductory section can be read to establish a common framework and terminology for discussing nonprofit-business alliances. For greater depth you may decide to read "The Strategic Benefits of Alliances," an introductory chapter in James Austin's book *The Collaboration Challenge.* For a lively and accessible introduction to successful nonprofit-business alliances, you may wish to view all or part of the companion resource *Meeting the Collaboration Challenge Video,* which illustrates a range of examples. Some are alliances of small and medium-sized nonprofits and local businesses; others are larger-scale alliances involving national nonprofit initiatives, Fortune 500 companies, and multiple partners. Appendix E in this workbook contains capsule descriptions of the five alliances presented in the video. The process options for Phases One, Two, and Three tell you which sections of the video best illustrate the relevant aspects of alliance development.

Appendix F in this workbook suggests further resources. This resource list is also available on the Drucker Foundation Web site [drucker.org/collaboration/], where it is periodically updated. This site also provides this workbook in a downloadable format and additional current resources for meeting the collaboration challenge, including information about related workshops.

Relationships between nonprofit organizations and businesses are becoming increasingly complex and strategic. They are migrating from charitable relationships between benevolent donors and grateful recipients to varied alliances that create diverse benefits for both partners and added value for communities. Today there is growing interest in the evolving range of partnerships, alliances, ventures, and collaborations between nonprofit organizations and businesses. These relationships result from opportunities and careful planning. To lead beyond the walls, nonprofit organizations need to be ready both to respond to serendipity and to seek out business partners systematically to develop alliances that further their missions.

The Range of Nonprofit-Business Relationships

The types of relationships between businesses and nonprofit organizations are evolving, as is the language that describes them. Most familiar are *contributions* of money and goods and *sponsorships* of events, activities, publications, and other products. These relationships provide goodwill for businesses and funds for nonprofit organizations. Businesses continue to encourage employees to *volunteer* with nonprofit organizations as board members, as fundraisers, in developing and delivering programs, and by providing pro bono technical expertise. Many nonprofit organizations regularly provide employee *services under contract* to businesses, in areas including child care, health, education, and job training and readiness.

Cause-related marketing has become increasingly familiar as businesses contribute a portion of revenue generated by specific marketing activities to the nonprofit organizations featured in those campaigns. Businesses and nonprofits are also joining in *social marketing* projects designed to create social benefits or behavioral change. Nonprofit organizations are arranging *licensing and "branding" agreements* in which businesses pay to use nonprofits' names, logos and images to enhance the businesses' marketing activities and the nonprofits' visibility and finances. And some nonprofit *entrepreneurs* are partnering with businesses in *social enterprises* to generate surplus revenues for nonprofits from creating, testing, distributing, or selling services and products.

Businesses' Benefits

The growth and the variety of relationships between businesses and nonprofit organizations are compelling evidence that businesses are obtaining benefits beyond the satisfactions of traditional philanthropy. These benefits are real and include generating and enhancing business opportunities, strengthening human resource management and the corporate culture, and supporting corporate strategies through community improvement.

A strategic alliance with a nonprofit organization can help *generate business* by enhancing a company's reputation, building goodwill, and strengthening its image. Such alliances can also expand a business's network, markets, and access to key customer groups. Alliance projects can provide arenas for developing and testing the business's products, services, and innovations.

As an expression of corporate values and a source of opportunities for community service, a strategic alliance with a nonprofit organization can *strengthen human resource management and corporate culture.* Alliance activities can:

- Enhance employee motivation, morale, loyalty, and retention.
- Foster empathy and caring that reinforce a focus on service.
- Expand opportunities for employees to practice leadership and management.
- Strengthen the organizational "glue" created by common values.
- Illuminate individuals' capabilities, values, and attitudes.
- Increase the organization's ability to attract potential employees.

Finally, *community improvement* has increasingly become part of corporate strategy. Alliances with nonprofit organizations provide opportunities for businesses to lead beyond the walls. Businesses can fulfill civic responsibilities and strengthen business conditions through positive impact on communities while simultaneously enhancing their images.

Nonprofit Organizations' Assets and Benefits

Nonprofit organizations are recognizing that their own broad range of *assets and capabilities* produces these benefits for businesses. Strategic alliances depend on nonprofits' powerful *missions* and strong *public images, access* to customers and markets, extensive *communication and distribution systems, relationships* with community leaders and other influential people, organizational *expertise* and *programs,* and other assets.

Through alliances with businesses, nonprofit organizations are realizing a broad range of *benefits for their customers* as well as for their organizational infrastructure and operations. These benefits come from relationships not only with those who manage businesses' philanthropic contributions but also with those in marketing, product development, human resources, public relations, and other business units. The benefits nonprofit organizations can realize range from *program innovation and delivery* to *revenues* and *goods,* from *people* to *facilities,* and from *publicity* to *information*. Nonprofit organizations can increase *public awareness* of issues and causes and achieve greater *organizational visibility* through alliances' public relations and marketing communications. Businesses can also provide *experts' pro bono assistance* and *access to other businesses and influential people* to expand nonprofit organizations' contacts.

Meeting the Challenge

The evolving range of relationships between nonprofit organizations and businesses presents opportunities for mutual benefits and results beyond those any organization or any sector could achieve alone. By meeting the collaboration challenge, nonprofit leaders can realize numerous benefits for their organizations and the communities they serve.

Prepare Your Nonprofit Organization to Meet the Collaboration Challenge

WORKSHEETS

1. Identify Assets and Capabilities Your Nonprofit Might Provide in Alliances

2. Determine Benefits Your Nonprofit Might Seek in Alliances

3. Review Your Nonprofit's Strategic Goals and Readiness for Developing Alliances

4. Delegate Responsibilities for Guiding Alliance Development

5. List Your Nonprofit's Current Relationships with Businesses

Process options for
PREPARING YOUR ORGANIZATION

Once your nonprofit organization becomes interested in strategic alliances with businesses, a systematic process can prepare the board and staff for meeting the challenges involved. This process can help your nonprofit develop effective alliances and incorporate alliance development into the broader processes of improving effectiveness, resource development, and strategic planning. Phase One is designed to ensure that alliances with businesses are based on a sound foundation that

- Acknowledges the assets and capabilities your nonprofit can provide to businesses (Worksheet 1).
- Provides benefits for your customers and furthers your mission (Worksheet 2).
- Aligns with your strategic goals and is supported by your governance, management, and organizational practices (Worksheet 3).
- Is guided by clear delegation of responsibilities within policy guidelines (Worksheet 4).
- Allows you to build on your nonprofit's current relationships with businesses (Worksheet 5).

This phase presents opportunities to strengthen the total organization's appreciation of what it can provide in alliances with businesses, what it can gain from these alliances, and what organizational capacity is necessary to create and manage alliances effectively. Governance support (Worksheet 3) and policy guidelines (Worksheet 4) are board responsibilities. However, it is best to be inclusive during this preparation phase and to provide opportunities for discussion with the board, volunteers, and staff.

The worksheets that follow can be used to organize individual input in advance of a meeting or retreat, prepare people for discussions, or structure individual and group work. An attractive option may be to conduct an inclusive two- to three-hour session that begins with the *Meeting the Collaboration Challenge Video*, showing the full thirty minutes or just the first two examples ("The Fox Cities Children's Museum and Roxanne's Doll Shop" and "City Year and Timberland"). The video examples provide an inspirational and instructive foundation for using Worksheets 1 and 2 to focus on your own nonprofit. Board members, volunteers, and staff can then consider Worksheets 3, 4, and 5 together, or this work can be delegated as appropriate.

Note: When necessary throughout your use of this workbook, please make additional copies of the worksheets provided.

Identify Assets and Capabilities Your Nonprofit Might Provide in Alliances

Building on the assets and capabilities of both partners, successful strategic alliances between nonprofit organizations and businesses provide benefits to both. Nonprofits seek benefits that will further their missions, serve their customers, strengthen their organizations, and achieve desired results: **changed lives and changed conditions.** In exchange, businesses seek a range of benefits, from enhancing business opportunities to strengthening human resource management to supporting corporate strategies through community improvement.

To prepare for developing effective alliances with businesses, identify the assets and capabilities your nonprofit possesses that may be valuable to businesses. By identifying what your nonprofit can provide alliance partners, you can also determine what types of businesses are most likely to value an alliance with your organization.

Read the following list of assets and capabilities on which nonprofit organizations build alliances with businesses. Briefly describe your organization's assets and capabilities, and indicate the types of businesses (or specific businesses) that are likely to value them.

Assets and Capabilities of Nonprofit Organizations	Our Nonprofit's Assets and Capabilities	Businesses Likely to Value Our Organization
Powerful mission: a compelling purpose, the organization's reason for being		
Strong presence: a well-known name, credibility, excellent reputation, attractive logo		
Access to potential customers or markets for sales, product development, and testing		

Assets and Capabilities of Nonprofit Organizations	*Our Nonprofit's Assets and Capabilities*	*Businesses Likely to Value Our Organization*
Extensive communication or distribution systems		
Organizational expertise in job training, child care, research, and so forth		
Programs and projects: arts programs, health services, environmental education, and so forth		
Volunteer opportunities: individual and team, short-term and long-term		
Ability to provide recognition, endorsement, or awards		
Access to potential employees to work for a business		
Well-known, respected leaders or spokespersons		

Assets and Capabilities of Nonprofit Organizations	Our Nonprofit's Assets and Capabilities	Businesses Likely to Value Our Organization
Access to community leaders and influential people or organizations		
Staff and volunteer skills and expertise		
Fundraising and financial capacity		
Facilities or equipment		
Products for use as incentives or giveaways: books, informational pamphlets, museum replicas, and so forth		
Other:		
Other:		

What, if anything, should we do to clarify and strengthen the assets and capabilities our organization can bring to alliances with businesses?

Additional notes:

Determine Benefits Your Nonprofit Might Seek in Alliances

Successful alliances with businesses provide valuable benefits to nonprofit organizations and the communities they serve. Clarity about what benefits your nonprofit is seeking through alliances helps you focus on partners most likely to provide these benefits.

Begin by rating most highly those benefits that will further your organization's mission and are most valued by your primary customers—**those whose lives are changed through the organization's work.** Also consider additional benefits to the organization. Then specify the **resources, recognition,** and **relationships** your nonprofit should seek, and identify businesses that might provide them.

Read the following list of benefits that nonprofits receive in strategic alliances with businesses. Rate how important each type of benefit would be to your organization. For those you rate 3, 4, or 5, briefly describe the specific benefits your nonprofit might seek (such as kinds of services, types of volunteers, and a target amount of funds), and indicate what types of businesses (or specific businesses) might provide them.

Benefits from Business Alliances	Importance (Circle One: 5 = Extremely Important; 1 = Not at All Important; DK = Don't Know)	Specific Benefits Our Nonprofit Might Seek and Businesses That Might Provide Them
Resources		
Program services: services that are valued by our primary customers and that further our mission	5 4 3 2 1 DK	
Knowledge: information that is helpful to our primary customers or that is useful to our organization	5 4 3 2 1 DK	

Benefits from Business Alliances	*Importance (Circle One: 5 = Extremely Important; 1 = Not at All Important; DK = Don't Know)*	*Specific Benefits Our Nonprofit Might Seek and Businesses That Might Provide Them*
Revenue: income from donations, grants, cause-related marketing proceeds, or revenues from contracts or fees that exceed performance costs	5 4 3 2 1 DK	
People: volunteers serving as board members, event participants, fundraisers, or service providers	5 4 3 2 1 DK	
Facilities: free or discounted access to or donations of buildings or other facilities for use by our customers or our organization	5 4 3 2 1 DK	
Goods: free or discounted items for distribution to our customers or for use or sale by our organization	5 4 3 2 1 DK	

Recognition

Issue awareness: expanded distribution of messages or information (often through public relations and marketing communications)	5 4 3 2 1 DK	

Benefits from Business Alliances	Importance (Circle One: 5 = Extremely Important; 1 = Not at All Important; DK = Don't Know)	Specific Benefits Our Nonprofit Might Seek and Businesses That Might Provide Them
Visibility: distinctive positioning or image building for our organization or our cause (often through public relations and marketing communications)	5 4 3 2 1 DK	

Relationships

Experts: pro bono assistance for our organization and our primary customers (often with technological, financial, scientific, research, communication, or legal issues)	5 4 3 2 1 DK	
Introductions to other businesses and influential people and groups: access to new sources of benefits for our customers and our organization	5 4 3 2 1 DK	

Other

Specify other:	5 4 3 2 1 DK	
Specify other:	5 4 3 2 1 DK	

What, if anything, should we do to clarify and rate the benefits our organization might seek from businesses?

Additional notes:

Review Your Nonprofit's Strategic Goals and Readiness for Developing Alliances

Alliances with businesses are part of the mix of strategies and tactics that effective nonprofit organizations employ to serve their customers, reach their goals, and achieve desired results. Taken together, a nonprofit's strategic goals are the board-approved vision of the desired future of the organization. Within that framework, board members, volunteers, and staff can examine how alliances fit and can set objectives for alliance projects.

Successful alliances between nonprofits and businesses require that nonprofits have effective leadership and management, high-quality programs, sound finances, and organizational practices open to entrepreneurial activities. Although effective alliances can help strengthen these fundamental organizational capacities, nonprofits need to have a solid foundation on which to build.

In light of opportunities to develop strategic alliances with businesses, your nonprofit should revisit its mission and strategic goals, consider objectives that might involve alliances, and assess its readiness to pursue them. Your nonprofit can then decide how to increase its capability in any areas and whether to proceed to develop alliances or to wait until improvements are made.

Write your nonprofit's mission, and then address the following questions about your nonprofit's strategic goals and organizational readiness, providing examples wherever possible.

Organization's mission:

	Our Nonprofit's Examples	*Comments and Concerns*
Strategic goals: What aspects of our vision for the organization's future can alliances help us realize?		
Effective governance: In what ways does our board demonstrate its capacity to establish sound policy, set clear direction, make timely decisions, delegate appropriately, and appraise performance?		

Our Nonprofit's Examples   *Comments and Concerns*

Effective management: In what ways do we demonstrate our ability to systematically plan, implement, and evaluate major initiatives?

Quality programs: What are the programs and services that demonstrate our organization's ability to achieve results?

Sound finances: In what ways is alliance development integrated with our overall resource development activities? Do we have sound financial systems so that alliances with businesses can be managed effectively?

Positive organizational culture: How have we demonstrated an openness to entrepreneurial activities, including seeking new opportunities, welcoming challenges, investing in new initiatives, undertaking reasonable risks, and learning from our experiences, whether or not they are successful?

Given our answers to these questions, how ready is our nonprofit to develop strategic alliances with businesses?

What, if anything, should our nonprofit undertake to strengthen its capability to develop and manage alliances (such as board, volunteer, and staff training or a resource development or strategic planning process)?

Should we begin developing strategic alliances while we strengthen our capabilities, or should we wait for specific improvements?

If we begin developing strategic alliances, how should we limit, if at all, the number or scope of alliance projects given our current organizational capacity?

Delegate Responsibilities for Guiding Alliance Development

Developing and managing strategic alliances with businesses involves a range of tasks, from the exploration of specific alliance options through planning alliance activities to periodic review of the entire alliance portfolio. These responsibilities are often guided by a small task group of board and staff members, usually led by the chief executive or an appointed executive staff member and a board member. These groups tend to include people experienced in resource development, project management, marketing, finance, public relations, and communications, as well as those with contacts in the business community. (Sometimes consultants are retained to provide planning or decision-making facilitation or expert advice on capacity building or alliance development.) This task group is responsible for regular communication about alliance development and for seeking governance and management attention whenever appropriate.

Because of the many questions that can arise regarding relationships between nonprofits and businesses, nonprofit boards need to set parameters on ethical matters such as conflicts of interest, product endorsements, and acceptable types of business partners and practices. Additional policy areas may also be addressed. It is a governance responsibility to make sure your nonprofit has adequate guidelines for developing strategic alliances. Appendix D presents a summary of nonprofit policy areas related to alliances and a sample policy statement.

At this point it is important to decide who should undertake the responsibilities for developing alliances with businesses, determine what policy guidelines are needed, and define next steps.

Summarize your nonprofit's answers to the following questions to delegate responsibilities for guiding alliance development.

Questions About Guiding Alliance Development	Suggestions for Our Nonprofit	Comments
Who should be responsible for guiding alliance development in our organization?		

Questions About Guiding Alliance Development	*Suggestions for Our Nonprofit*	*Comments*
Should a special group be appointed for any or all of the tasks involved? If so, what areas of expertise or individuals should be included?		
Should we consider contractors or consultants in any roles?		
What policies do we have and what guidelines do we need to set for developing strategic alliances?		
What next steps should we take to clearly delegate alliance development responsibilities?		

List Your Nonprofit's Current Relationships with Businesses

Most nonprofit organizations have many existing commercial relationships with businesses as well as philanthropic and other alliances. Nonprofits purchase supplies, equipment, facilities, and utilities. They use professional services from banks, accountants, lawyers, insurance companies, and others. Nonprofits' transactions with for-profit businesses can involve market rates or discounted fees, as well as donated goods, facilities, and services.

Some businesses develop relationships with nonprofits because their employees volunteer with these nonprofits. Many nonprofits have a range of philanthropic relationships, in which they receive financial contributions from businesses through gifts and events, that are not perceived as strategic alliances.

When nonprofits consider developing strategic alliances, their existing relationships with businesses can provide opportunities for expanding activities and mutual benefits. Therefore an inventory of your current relationships with businesses is an excellent way to begin identifying potential partners for strategic alliances.

To identify your nonprofit's potential strategic alliances, list the businesses with which you currently have relationships, and briefly characterize each relationship.

Business	*Character of Current Relationship*
1.	
2.	
3.	
4.	
5.	
6.	

Plan Your Nonprofit Organization's Strategic Alliances with Businesses

WORKSHEETS

6. Map Your Nonprofit's Business Relationships on the Collaboration Continuum

7. Research Each Potential Alliance to Assess Strategic Fit and Opportunities

8. Identify Other Businesses with Which Your Nonprofit Might Create Alliances

9. Design a Marketing Approach for Each Potential Alliance

Process options for
PLANNING ALLIANCES

Once you have determined that your nonprofit organization is ready to develop strategic alliances with businesses, planning is necessary to determine which alliances you will actively pursue. Phase Two gives you the opportunity to explore strategic development of current relationships, to identify other potential business partners, and to market alliances with the businesses most likely to provide your customers and your organization with the benefits they seek.

The specific individuals, task force, or team identified to guide alliance development (Worksheet 4) now take responsibility for planning alliances. Coordination with other resource development activities is especially important. Depending on your organization's size and practices, this phase may benefit from additional volunteers and staff who can bring information and insights to

- Thinking strategically about your nonprofit's current relationships with businesses and their alliance potential (Worksheets 6 and 7)
- Identifying new partners (Worksheet 8) and assessing their alliance potential with your nonprofit (Worksheet 7)
- Designing marketing approaches for each alliance your nonprofit decides to pursue (Worksheet 9)

The second and third nonprofit-business alliances ("City Year and Timberland" and "The Stairstep Initiative and General Mills and Glory Foods") in the *Meeting the Collaboration Challenge Video* provide exciting examples of the concepts in Worksheets 6 and 7, and the fourth video example ("Salvation Army Golden Diners and Bill's Restaurant") is especially useful for highlighting the importance of marketing (Worksheet 9). In addition, you may wish to review Chapters Two, Three, Four, and Five in James Austin's book *The Collaboration Challenge* for more information about ensuring strategic fit, making connections, and generating value.

Map Your Nonprofit's Business Relationships on the Collaboration Continuum

The **Collaboration Continuum** is a framework for thinking strategically about relationships between nonprofit organizations and businesses. Developed by James Austin and adapted here from his book *The Collaboration Challenge,* it consists of three stages:

Philanthropic ····· ←→ ····· **Transactional** ····· ←→ ····· **Integrative**

Philanthropic relationships exist between nonprofit organizations and their donors, who provide tangible resources (such as money or goods) in exchange for intangible benefits from the nonprofit (such as enhanced reputation or fulfillment of the desire to help others). Generally, these interactions and activities are handled by the nonprofit's development volunteers and staff and the business's corporate contributions staff. Strategic value is usually determined by considering the resources nonprofits gain that they can use to achieve desired results and the opportunities businesses gain to support their communities and meet their philanthropic objectives.

Transactional relationships consist of exchanges of resources through specific activities, such as event sponsorship, licensing, service contracts, volunteer programs, and cause-related marketing. In comparison with the philanthropic stage, the level of interaction usually intensifies, relationship management becomes more complex, and a broader sense of partnership may develop. This stage tends to involve the business's operating staff (for example, product development and marketing, human resources, finance) and more nonprofit staff from a range of areas. These relationships are usually perceived by both the business and nonprofit partners as having greater strategic value than philanthropic relationships.

Integrative relationships are characterized by joint activities or ventures that are perceived as having major strategic value by both the business and the nonprofit organization. These partnerships usually reflect strong understanding of each other's values, engage top leadership and numerous staff, and involve exploration and creation of new and expanded benefits for both partners. In this stage, formal processes and procedures are developed to handle complex management requirements, and each partner's values and practices are often affected by the other's.

Movement along the Collaboration Continuum generally results from deliberate decisions by the nonprofit organization and the business to modify the scope of their relationship. Some relationships begin at the transactional or integrative stages, and many are hybrids that include philanthropic components along with other projects.

Most nonprofits are strengthened by having a diversified resource base, including a variety of relationships with businesses. Your organization can benefit by assessing current relationships with businesses and planning whether and how to move them on the Collaboration Continuum.

Review Worksheet 5 and the list of businesses with which your organization currently has relationships and place a check (✓) next to those businesses you believe have the most promising alliance potential.

Then, below, fill in the name of each prospective alliance partner, and mark an "X" where you currently find your relationship with that business along the Collaboration Continuum.

Business *(fill in):* _____

Philanthropic	Transactional	Integrative

Business: _____

Philanthropic	Transactional	Integrative

Business: _____

Philanthropic	Transactional	Integrative

Business: _____

Philanthropic	Transactional	Integrative

Business: _____

Philanthropic	Transactional	Integrative

Research Each Potential Alliance to Assess Strategic Fit and Opportunities

Successful alliances between nonprofit organizations and businesses depend on the partners' strategic fit: **their compatibility and ability to develop mutually beneficial projects.** Research, even regarding businesses with which a nonprofit already has relationships, helps the nonprofit assess strategic fit, opportunities to create mutual benefits, and the costs and risks that may be involved in an alliance. Research may also help to generate ideas about potential alliance projects.

Businesses increasingly release information that describes their missions, values, goals, product and service lines, reputations, and plans. You may wish to review public relations materials, including annual and community relations reports, as well as documents that businesses are required to file with government agencies. You may also inquire into businesses' alliances with other nonprofit organizations and noteworthy business practices.

Some of the most valuable research is conducted by informal networking, especially through your nonprofit's business volunteers. Trade and general interest media carry current news about businesses, including frequent reports on cause-related marketing and other highly visible alliance activities. Businesses' own Web sites are rich sources of information, and the Internet is making it easier to search for local, regional, national, and international business information. Local libraries and print directories continue to be valuable resources. The Drucker Foundation Web site [drucker.org/collaboration/] provides a list of Web sites for business research.

Using your knowledge of your nonprofit's research, respond to the following questions for each business you identified as having promising alliance potential.

Business: _____

How might our mission and values attract and be compatible with this business? Are there areas where our ethics or values might conflict with those of the business?

How might an alliance with this business serve our primary customers and the community? What benefits might this alliance provide to help our nonprofit further its mission? Would this alliance provide services our primary customers value? Would this alliance benefit our nonprofit's operations?

How might this alliance contribute to the business's strategy? Would it help generate business? Enhance the company's image? Reach new markets? Support human resource development? Strengthen corporate culture? Improve business and social conditions in the community?

What assets and capabilities might be exchanged in this alliance? What might our nonprofit provide and expect to receive? What might this business provide and expect to receive?

How will this alliance be incorporated into our nonprofit's operating plan? What costs might this alliance involve? How much leadership and management time would this alliance project require from each partner? What other investments of resources might be required?

What risks might this alliance involve? What risks to each other's reputation? What financial risks?

Given this preliminary assessment, does this business have strong potential for a strategic alliance that will further our nonprofit's mission?

If so, note any ideas for alliance projects with this business.

If this business does not seem to have strong alliance potential and our nonprofit already has a relationship with this business, should our nonprofit maintain, expand, narrow, or abandon this relationship?

Identify Other Businesses with Which Your Nonprofit Might Create Alliances

Although it is generally easiest and fastest for a nonprofit organization to develop alliances through existing relationships with businesses, many nonprofit organizations seek out additional businesses for alliances. Most nonprofits conduct their own research and outreach activities to find new alliance partners. Potential partners are sometimes found through **market-makers,** including public relations, advertising, and communications firms that develop sponsorships, cause-related marketing programs, and image campaigns. There are also consulting groups that specialize in facilitating partner identification and alliance development for nonprofit organizations.

If your nonprofit wants alliance benefits that are not likely to come from businesses with which it already has relationships, it is best to search systematically for other alliance partners using well-defined criteria. Partner search criteria may include type of industry, mission and values, location, size, financial performance, reputation, philanthropic interests, and track record with other nonprofit alliances. You may wish to refer back to Worksheet 7 for a description of information sources and research approaches.

After reviewing benefit areas you rated highly (3, 4, or 5) on Worksheet 2, describe as specifically as possible those benefits that are *not* likely to be provided by your nonprofit's current business partners. Then, after reviewing your notes on Worksheet 1 about businesses that might value an alliance with your nonprofit, define criteria for identifying businesses that might provide the benefits you seek. Next, using your research, list specific businesses that meet these criteria. Finally, rank the businesses according to the importance of the benefits they may provide and the likelihood of their interest in developing an alliance with your nonprofit.

| | *Potential Business Partner* | | |
| *Benefits Sought* | *Selection Criteria* | *Specific Businesses* | *Rank* |

1.

2.

Benefits Sought	Potential Business Partner Selection Criteria	Specific Businesses	Rank
3.			
4.			
5.			
6.			

Return to Worksheet 7 to assess strategic fit and alliance opportunities for businesses that have promising alliance potential.

Design a Marketing Approach for Each Potential Alliance

Once a nonprofit organization has determined that a business is an attractive candidate for an alliance, the nonprofit needs to gain that business's commitment to develop an alliance. Viewing each business as a customer, the nonprofit markets an alliance to that prospective partner.

To design an effective marketing approach for each potential partner, plan how to connect with key people in the business, understand the business's needs, foster interest in possible alliance projects, and follow up in a timely, responsive, and persistent manner.

To prepare for marketing each potential alliance, respond to the following questions.

Business: _____

Steps	*Our Marketing Approach*
Plan how to identify business contacts	
If someone associated with our nonprofit has a strong contact within the business, who is the person and how should the business best be approached?	
or	
If no one in our nonprofit has a strong contact within the business, how will we find one? Do we know others who may have strong contacts or information? Are there business publications or associations that may provide names? Are there logical people in the business to "cold call" (to serve as contacts themselves or to recommend others we might approach)?	

Steps	*Our Marketing Approach*

Plan the initial discussion

In the light of our research and responses to Worksheet 7 on strategic fit and opportunities, how will our nonprofit make the case that a meeting to explore a potential alliance would be worthwhile?

Who in our nonprofit should conduct this discussion with the business representative?

Plan the initial meeting

Considering our responses to Worksheet 7, what key points should we make during the initial meeting to build the business's interest in a potential alliance?

Who in our nonprofit should plan this meeting? Should the meeting be planned jointly with someone inside the business? Who from our nonprofit should participate in this meeting?

Plan to share information and materials

What do we want the business to understand about our nonprofit and the potential benefits to the business? What materials, if any, should be presented either before or during the initial meeting, such as

- General materials (annual reports, news articles, and brochures)

- A fact sheet highlighting our nonprofit's assets and capabilities

Steps	*Our Marketing Approach*

• A one-page concept paper outlining potential benefits to the business and ideas for alliance projects

What questions should be asked to learn more about the business, its needs, and its strategies?

Plan next steps and follow-up

What immediate expressions of interest or commitment do we wish to obtain from the business, and what next steps should be agreed on, such as

• Additional meetings

• Other opportunities to build mutual understanding and develop ideas for the potential alliance

Unless the business explicitly precludes further contact, how will our nonprofit demonstrate interest and responsiveness?

Develop Strategic Alliances with Businesses

WORKSHEETS

10. Develop the Purpose and Fit Statement for Each Alliance

11. Develop the Management Plan for Each Alliance

Process options for
DEVELOPING ALLIANCES

Once your nonprofit organization and a business have established mutual interest in an alliance, your nonprofit is ready to work together with the business partner to develop clear expectations about alliance projects and to determine how these projects will contribute strategic benefits to each organization. During this phase you collaborate with your alliance partner to design projects and agree on the alliance management plan.

This phase requires the focused time and energy of both the nonprofit organization and the business so the partners can successfully

- Develop the overall strategic framework for the alliance (Worksheet 10)
- Determine how alliance projects will be managed for performance (Worksheet 11)

The specific individuals, task force, or team identified to guide alliance development (Worksheet 4) may continue to lead alliance development, and a *relationship manager* from each organization should be identified at this stage to ensure effective coordination. Depending on the scope of the proposed alliance and your organizational practices, this phase may involve a substantial number of volunteers and staff. Some complex issues may also require the participation of legal or other expert counsel.

Worksheets 10 and 11 are designed to be completed together by alliance partners. They can also be used in advance to guide your nonprofit organization's thinking, to consider how the partner may respond, and to prepare for discussion. The fifth example in the *Meeting the Collaboration Challenge Video* ("The Computer Clubhouse and Intel") may provide useful insights and motivation to help your nonprofit focus on the management challenges addressed in Worksheet 11. In addition, you may wish to review Chapter Eight, on guidelines for collaborating successfully, in James Austin's *The Collaboration Challenge*.

Develop the Purpose and Fit Statement for Each Alliance

Successful alliances between nonprofit organizations and businesses reflect mutual understanding of the alliance's strategic fit and rely on the partners' ability to develop opportunities into projects that provide significant benefits. The partners work together to design the alliance in order to meet each organization's objectives and contribute strategic value to both.

At this point, meet with your nonprofit organization's business alliance partner and establish clear, mutual expectations about the alliance's purpose and fit. Written agreements are recommended to avoid misunderstandings and provide a basis for future appraisal, though many successful alliances rely on oral agreements, with written documents limited to legal issues.

After reviewing your assessment of the strategic fit and opportunities for an alliance with a business (Worksheet 7), work jointly with your partner to develop a purpose and fit statement.

STRATEGIC ALLIANCE PURPOSE AND FIT STATEMENT

between

Business: _____

Nonprofit organization: _____

Nonprofit's mission and values: Business's mission and values:

Nonprofit's assets and capabilities   Business's assets and capabilities
invested in this alliance: invested in this alliance:

Nonprofit's objectives for this alliance:

Business's objectives for this alliance:

Contribution to the nonprofit's strategy:

Contribution to the business's strategy:

Alliance project activities:

Develop the Management Plan for Each Alliance

Successful strategic alliances between nonprofits and businesses depend on effective management by both organizations. This mutual commitment to performance can be reinforced by partners working together to develop the management plan for the alliance.

In meetings with your alliance partner, work together to establish clear mutual expectations. Written agreements help avoid misunderstandings and provide a useful basis for future appraisals. However, many successful alliances rely on oral agreements and ongoing communication to identify and resolve management issues.

After completing the purpose and fit statement (Worksheet 10), work with your alliance partner to develop a management plan.

STRATEGIC ALLIANCE MANAGEMENT PLAN
between

Business: _____

Nonprofit organization: _____

How will the alliance capture sufficient attention among each partner's key leaders to achieve its objectives?

Whom will each partner appoint to serve as overall relationship manager(s) and the manager(s) of alliance projects?

How will the alliance be institutionalized in each partner organization's plans and practices to ensure continuity despite any personnel changes?

How will the alliance build mutual trust and commitment?

How will ongoing and effective communication about alliance projects be maintained between the partners, within each partner's organization, and with customers and others?

How often will the partners meet to appraise the alliance's progress and the partners' performance?

How will each partner continue to learn about the other in order to strengthen the alliance, explore opportunities, and develop innovations?

Renew Your Nonprofit Organization's Strategic Alliances with Businesses

WORKSHEETS

12. Prepare for Alliance Appraisal

13. Update Your Nonprofit's Operating Plan

14. Review Your Nonprofit's Portfolio of Alliances

Process options for

ALLIANCE APPRAISAL AND RENEWAL

Once your nonprofit organization is engaged in strategic alliances with businesses, it is important to appraise and renew each alliance separately and review all your alliances together as a portfolio. These processes allow your nonprofit to maximize the benefits of alliances, update its operating plan, and incorporate alliances into long-range planning. During this phase, your nonprofit

- Plans independently for appraisal with its alliance partner (Worksheet 12) and then works with its partner to make further plans together
- Updates its operating plan to reflect renewed alliances (Worksheet 13)
- Reviews its portfolio of alliances with businesses, and considers how alliances should be incorporated in long-range plans (Worksheet 14)

Alliance relationship managers generally play a key role in the appraisal process, which can also include volunteers and staff who have been directly involved in alliance projects. The specific individuals, task force, or team identified to guide alliance development for your nonprofit (Worksheet 4) may also participate in preparing for the appraisal of each alliance as well as the review of your nonprofit's total portfolio of alliances with businesses. This is an excellent time to get feedback from your customers—those the alliances are designed to benefit. The insights of customers, volunteers, and staff are helpful when completing Worksheet 12 in preparation for your nonprofit's meeting with its alliance partner to appraise and, if mutually appropriate, renew the alliance.

After your nonprofit completes the alliance appraisal with its partner, the decision will be made whether to maintain, expand, narrow, or abandon the alliance. Where appropriate, the alliance partners revise their initial purpose and fit statement (Worksheet 10) and management plan (Worksheet 11). Worksheet 13 provides a format for summarizing this work and the implications for updating your nonprofit's operating plan.

Finally, Worksheet 14 is designed to help your nonprofit review its portfolio of alliances with businesses for incorporation into long-range organizational assessment and strategic planning. The individuals, task force, or team identified to guide alliance development (Worksheet 4) often provide the leadership to address Worksheet 14. In addition to completing this worksheet, you may want to review pages 140 to 144 in James Austin's *The Collaboration Challenge* for more about strategic management of alliance portfolios.

Prepare for Alliance Appraisal

Successful strategic alliances usually grow more successful when both partners commit themselves to appraising the alliance, exploring opportunities, developing innovations, and renewing the partnership periodically. Appraisal provides the opportunity to mark progress, review the purpose and fit statement and the management plan, reflect on what each partner is learning about developing an effective alliance, and make further plans. Appraisal is part of the alliance management plan (Worksheet 11) and takes place at intervals appropriate to each alliance. The outcomes of the appraisal process are incorporated into the nonprofit's regular processes for updating operating and long-range plans.

To prepare for an appraisal meeting with your nonprofit's alliance partner, first assess the alliance's performance to date and its potential in the next one to three years. Then, consider how the alliance can provide the greatest benefits within your organization's governance and management capacity. Finally, plan for your nonprofit's meeting with its alliance partner to determine whether to maintain, expand, narrow, or abandon this alliance.

After reviewing the alliance's purpose and fit statement (Worksheet 10) and management plan (Worksheet 11), consider the following to prepare for an appraisal meeting with your nonprofit's alliance partner.

Business: _____

	How Are Our Expectations Being Met, Not Being Met, Changed, or Exceeded?	*How Do We Think Our Partner's Expectations Are Being Met, Not Being Met, Changed, or Exceeded?*
The strategic fit between the partners		
Objectives for the alliance		

	How Are Our Expectations Being Met, Not Being Met, Changed, or Exceeded?	*How Do We Think Our Partner's Expectations Are Being Met, Not Being Met, Changed, or Exceeded?*
Contributions to strategies		
The management plan		

Is this alliance significantly benefiting our customers and furthering our mission? If so, how?

Is this alliance producing unexpected benefits for either or both partners? If so, what are they?

Do the alliance's benefits for our customers and our nonprofit justify its costs? In what ways?

What are we learning about developing a more effective alliance with this partner?

Given this preliminary review:

Based on our organizational capability, does our nonprofit want to maintain, expand, narrow, or abandon this alliance?

Over the next one to three years, where might our nonprofit organization want to move the alliance on the continuum? Mark a ★ at the point to which you want this alliance to move.

Philanthropic   Transactional   Integrative

Therefore, what are our nonprofit's objectives for the appraisal meeting with this alliance partner?

Who from our nonprofit should attend this meeting?

What next steps should we take to develop the agenda and materials for this meeting?

Update Your Nonprofit's Operating Plan

An effective alliance appraisal process results in the partners' mutual agreement to maintain, expand, narrow, or abandon the relationship. Even when an alliance has been successful, occasionally one of the partners decides it is no longer in its strategic interest to continue, and the partners work together to develop a mutually satisfactory end. Therefore, regardless of an alliance appraisal's outcome, the nonprofit needs to update its operating plan.

Following the appraisal process with your alliance partner, summarize this work and the implications for your nonprofit's operating plan. For example, the revised alliance plan may involve new costs, different allocations of leadership and management time, or investments of other resources.

Following the appraisal process, summarize the work and implications for your nonprofit's operating plan by responding to the following.

Business: _____

Nonprofit organization: _____

Alliance direction (maintain, expand, narrow, or abandon):

Contribution to our nonprofit's strategies and objectives:

Alliance project activities:

Benefits to our customers and our nonprofit:

Costs to our nonprofit:

- Financial

- Leadership and management time

- Other investments

What changes does this review suggest for our organization's annual operating plan?

Review Your Nonprofit's Portfolio of Alliances

Many effective nonprofit organizations revisit their missions and long-range plans every three to five years. These organizational self-assessment and strategic planning processes provide an opportunity to review the portfolio of alliances with businesses and determine how alliances should be employed in the nonprofit's long-range plan.

Nonprofit organizations that engage in alliances with businesses are sometimes involved in several simultaneously. Steps to review an alliance portfolio include listing current alliances with businesses, mapping these alliances on the Collaboration Continuum, and noting how these alliances have helped the nonprofit serve its customers, reach goals, and achieve desired results. These planning processes also provide an opportunity to scan current trends in the ways nonprofits and businesses succeed through strategic alliances.

A portfolio review allows you to acknowledge what your nonprofit organization is learning about meeting the collaboration challenge with businesses, examine whether you should strengthen organizational capacity to develop and manage alliances, and recommend alliance-related goals and objectives for your nonprofit's long-range plan.

To review your nonprofit's portfolio of alliances, use the following chart to list each alliance partner and the alliance's contribution to your nonprofit's strategies.

Alliance Partner	*Alliance's Contribution to Nonprofit's Strategy*
Business A:	
Business B:	
Business C:	
Business D:	
Business E:	
Business F:	

Then, using the most recent alliance appraisal (as reported on Worksheet 13), indicate each alliance's current position on the Collaboration Continuum below with the appropriate low-ercase letter (for example, mark an "a" for Business A) and each alliance's desired position in the next three to five years with a capital letter (for example, mark an "A" for Business A). Then address the questions that follow.

Philanthropic   Transactional   Integrative

How are strategic alliances with businesses helping our nonprofit organization to:

• Serve our customers?

• Reach our strategic goals?

• Achieve desired results?

What are our nonprofit organization's most significant challenges in developing and managing strategic alliances with businesses?

What are our nonprofit organization's most promising opportunities for developing and managing strategic alliances with businesses?

In what ways should our nonprofit strengthen its capacity to develop and manage alliances?

How should alliances with businesses be reflected in our nonprofit's long-range goals and objectives?

Afterword

Peter Drucker provides us with the big picture of the nonprofit organization's significance and indispensable role, today and tomorrow. "The more economy, money, and information become *global*, the more *community* will matter," notes Peter. "The leadership, competence, and management of the social sector nonprofit organization will thus largely determine the values, the vision, the cohesion, and the performance of the 21st century society."

There is a new energy as leaders of the future embrace the opportunities in this wider world. Social sector leaders must step to the fore and, employing the strength of nonprofit missions and values, operate as the "equal partner of business and government in developing responsible leaders, caring citizens, and a healthy, inclusive society."

Each alliance with a business that your nonprofit organization develops, carries out, and appraises can further your mission and enhance your capacity to lead beyond the walls. It is through alliances, partnerships, and collaborations that organizations across all sectors together build the inclusive, cohesive community that cares about all its people.

Definition of Terms

Alliances, partnerships, collaborations

Relationships that provide opportunities for mutual benefits and results beyond those any single organization or sector could realize alone.

Appraisal

A process for monitoring progress and achievement; a point at which plans are modified based on experience or changed conditions.

Customers

Those who must be satisfied for the organization to achieve results. Your nonprofit's *primary customer* is the person whose life is changed through the nonprofit's work. *Supporting customers* are volunteers, members, partners, funders, referral sources, employees, and others who must also be satisfied.

Customer value

That which satisfies customers' *needs* (physical and psychological well-being), *wants* (where, when, and how service is provided), and *aspirations* (desired long-term results).

Goals

A set of three to five overarching aspirations that taken together are the board's vision of the desired future of the organization.

Mission

Why the organization does what it does; the organization's reason for being, its purpose.

Objectives

Specific and measurable levels of achievement.

Operating plan

Management's annual plan, including objectives, action steps, accountabilities, resource allocations, and appraisal.

Performance	The total organization's progress and achievements.
Results	The organization's bottom line; defined in *changed conditions* and *changed lives*—people's behavior, circumstances, health, hopes, competence, or capacity. Results are always *outside* the organization.
Strategic fit	Partners' compatibility and ability to develop mutually beneficial projects.

The Seven C's: Questions for Partners

James Austin's *The Collaboration Challenge* presents the seven C's of strategic collaboration. The following, reproduced with permission from *The Collaboration Challenge*, are questions you can use to assess an alliance against the seven C's.

Connection with Purpose and People

- To what extent are individuals personally and emotionally connected to the social purpose of the collaboration?
- Have individuals been able to touch, feel, and see the social value of the collaboration?
- What level and what quality of interaction exist among senior leaders?
- To what extent do personal connections and interactions occur at other levels across the partnering organizations?
- How strong are interpersonal bonds?

Clarity of Purpose

- What is the purpose of the collaboration?
- Where does the relationship fall on the Collaboration Continuum (is it philanthropic, transactional, or integrative), and where does each partner want it to be?
- Have the partners escaped the gratefulness and charity syndrome?
- Do both partners have written collaboration purpose statements?
- Has each partner determined the different functions and relative importance of the partnerships already existing in its collaboration portfolio?

Congruency of mission, strategy, and values

- How well does each partner understand the other's business?
- What are the missions, strategies, and values of each partner?

- What are the areas of current and potential overlap?
- How can each partner help the other accomplish its mission?
- To what extent is the collaboration a strategic tool for each partner?
- Have the partners engaged in shared visioning about the future?

Creation of Value

- What resources of each partner are of value to the other?
- What specific benefits will accrue to each partner from the collaboration?
- Do benefits outweigh costs and risks?
- What social value can be generated by the alliance?
- What new resources, capabilities, and benefits can be created by the collaboration?
- Are resource and capability transfer two-way?
- Are benefits equitably balanced between the partners?
- Has the value exchange and creation depreciated? If so, to what extent?
- Can the Collaboration Value Construct be renewed and enhanced?
- Is it time to end the collaboration?

Communication Between Partners

- What level of respect and trust exists between the partners?
- Is communication open and frank, and is critical communication constructive?
- How is communication between the partners managed?
- Does each partner have a partner relationship manager?
- What channels and vehicles are used to communicate internally?
- Are there potential dissenters, and can they be converted?
- How does the alliance communicate externally?
- Do the partners have a coordinated external communication strategy and program?
- Is the partnership underpublicized?

Continual Learning

- What has each partner learned from the collaboration about how to work with another organization more effectively and create greater partner and social value?
- How has this learning been incorporated into the collaboration?
- Is there a process for routinely assessing learning from the collaboration?
- Is complacency stifling innovation?

Commitment to the Partnership

- What is the level of organizational commitment to the partnership, and how is this commitment demonstrated?

- What is the trend in investments (personal, financial, institutional) in the partnership?
- Are the partners' expectations of one another high?
- What is the composition of each partner's collaboration portfolio, and where does this alliance fit within those portfolios?
- Are the portfolios consistent with the partners' collaboration capacities?

Factors Influencing the Success of Collaboration

Following are the twenty factors that influence the success of collaborations formed by nonprofit organizations, government agencies, and other organizations.[1] The authors who identified these factors note: "Much of the research suggests that these factors can apply to collaborative efforts that link business organizations with nonprofit organizations as well."

1. Factors Related to the ENVIRONMENT
    A. *History of collaboration or cooperation in the community*

    A history of collaboration or cooperation exists in the community and offers the potential collaborative partners an understanding of the roles and expectations required in collaboration and enables them to trust the process.

    B. *Collaborative group seen as a legitimate leader in the community*

    The collaborative group (and by implication the agencies in the group) is perceived within the community as reliable and competent (at least related to the goals and activities it intends to accomplish.

    C. *Favorable political and social climate*

    Political leaders, opinion-makers, persons who control resources, and the general public support (or at least do not oppose) the mission of the collaborative group.

---

[1] Adapted from *Collaboration: What Makes It Work,* 2nd ed., by Paul W. Mattessich, Marta Murray-Close, and Barbara Monsey, copyright 2001, Amherst H. Wilder Foundation. Used with permission. For more information on Wilder Foundation publications, call 1-800-274-6024.

2. Factors Related to MEMBERSHIP CHARACTERISTICS

   A. *Mutual respect, understanding, and trust*

      Members of the collaborative group share an understanding and respect for each other and their respective organizations: how they operate, their cultural norms and values, their limitations, and their expectations.

   B. *Appropriate cross section of members*

      To the extent that they are needed, the collaborative group includes representatives from each segment of the community who will be affected by its activities.

   C. *Members see collaboration as in their self-interest*

      Collaborating partners believe that they will benefit from their involvement in the collaboration and that the advantages of membership will offset costs such as loss of autonomy and turf.

   D. *Ability to compromise*

      Collaborating partners are able to compromise, since the many decisions within a collaborative effort cannot possible fit the preferences of every member perfectly.

3. Factors Related to PROCESS AND STRUCTURE

   A. *Members share a stake in both process and outcome*

      Members of a collaborative group feel "ownership" of both the way the group works and the results or products of its work.

   B. *Multiple layers of participation*

      Every level (upper management, middle management, operations) within each partner organization has at least some representation and ongoing involvement in the collaborative initiative.

   C. *Flexibility*

      The collaborative group remains open to varied ways of organizing itself and accomplishing its work.

   D. *Development of clear roles and policy guidelines*

      The collaborating partners clearly understand their roles, rights, and responsibilities, and they understand how to carry out those responsibilities.

   E. *Adaptability*

      The collaborative group has the ability to sustain itself in the midst of major changes, even if it needs to change some major goals, members, etc., in order to deal with changing conditions.

   F. *Appropriate pace of development*

      The structure, resources, and activities of the collaborative group change over time to meet the needs of the group without overwhelming its capacity, at each point throughout the initiative.

4. Factors Related to COMMUNICATION

    A. *Open and frequent communication*

       Collaborative group members interact often, update one another, discuss issues openly, and convey all necessary information to one another and to people outside the group.

    B. *Established informal relationships and communication links*

       In addition to formal channels of communication, members establish personal connections (producing a better, more informed, and cohesive group working on a common project).

5. Factors Related to PURPOSE

    A. *Concrete, attainable goals and objectives*

       Goals and objectives of the collaborative group are clear to all partners, and can realistically be attained.

    B. *Shared vision*

       Collaborating partners have the same vision, with clearly agreed-upon mission, objectives, and strategy. The shared vision may exist at the outset of collaboration, or the partners may develop a vision as they work together.

    C. *Unique purpose*

       The mission and goals, or approach, of the collaborative group differ, at least in part, from the mission and goals, or approach, of the member organizations.

6. Factors Related to RESOURCES

    A. *Sufficient funds, staff, materials, and time*

       The collaborative group has an adequate, consistent financial base, along with the staff and materials needed to support its operations. It allows sufficient time to achieve its goals and includes time to nurture the collaboration.

    B. *Skilled leadership*

       The individual who provides leadership for the collaborative group has organizing and interpersonal skills, and carries out the role with fairness. Because of these characteristics (and others), the leader is granted respect or "legitimacy" by the collaborative partners.

Nonprofit Policies for Alliances with Businesses

It is important that each nonprofit board of directors determines the organization's position on policy issues commonly raised when participating in alliances with businesses. Developing strategic alliances with businesses often brings to the surface ethical questions regarding conflicts of interest, product endorsements, and acceptable business partners. These and other issues require consideration and the development of policy guidelines for prudent and timely organizational decision making.

This appendix presents nine policy areas related to alliances and a sample policy statement. The Drucker Foundation Web site [drucker.org/collaboration/] provides additional policy resources including links to sample policy statements.

The information following is provided solely for educational purposes and does not constitute legal advice. Your organization should seek legal counsel or other professional advice before adopting policies.

1. Mission and ethics: policies that address the nonprofit's position on the degree to which alliances must be congruent with mission and values. Also policies that address conflicts of interest.

Sample policy: *Values Congruence*

[Nonprofit] will have alliances involving only businesses, products, and services consistent with the values, principles, standards, and guidelines of [nonprofit]. Upon periodic review, the board of directors may prohibit [nonprofit] from entering into alliances with specific types of organizations engaged in activities judged to be harmful to the health or welfare of [nonprofit's] customers or otherwise in conflict with [nonprofit's] mission or values.

Other potential policies:
Mission congruence
Conflict of interest

2. Legal and liability protections: policies that ensure alliance activities will comply with public disclosure requirements, will not violate any legal constraints on nonprofit-business relationships, will not endanger tax-exempt status, and will not expose the organization to undue liability. May require formal alliance agreements with exit clauses.

   Potential policies:
   Public disclosure
   Liability protection
   Terms of agreement

3. Name and reputation protection: policies that require formal permission and set standards for use of the nonprofit's name, logo, service marks, and other identifying marks or messages. Will constrain relationships that could be judged to create negative perceptions of the organization or its cause.

   Potential policy:
   Name and brand protection

4. Endorsements: policies that establish whether the nonprofit will, explicitly or by conferring any certifications, endorse any businesses or their products or services and, if so, under what specific conditions.

   Potential policy:
   Endorsements

5. Exclusivity: policies that establish whether, and under what circumstances, a nonprofit will grant exclusivity in its alliance relationships with businesses.

   Potential policy:
   Exclusivity

6. Privacy and confidentiality: policies that outline privacy protections for the nonprofit's customers and confidentiality protections for the nonprofit and its alliance partners.

   Potential policy:
   Privacy and confidentiality

7. Due diligence: policies that establish the scope and requirements for research, cost-benefit analysis, and risk assessment regarding alliances. Defines authority and approval processes for making alliance agreements.

   Potential policy:
   Advance review and approval

8. Relationship management and appraisal: policies that define requirements and protocols for managing and evaluating alliances with businesses.

   Potential policy:
   Management and appraisal

9. Coordination with affiliates: policies for national, international, or other federated organizations that define the degree to which decisions regarding alliances with businesses are centralized or at the discretion of individual affiliates and how alliances will be managed across the organization.

   Potential policy:
   Coordination with affiliates

Alliance Examples in *Meeting the Collaboration Challenge Video*

Meeting the Collaboration Challenge Video
(Thirty minutes, VHS)

The *Meeting the Collaboration Challenge Video* presents five lively and inspiring examples of nonprofit-business alliances. Leaders of these alliances describe their partnerships' development and evolution. Earlier in this workbook, the process options for each phase suggested how the video can be used all at once or in segments to illustrate particular aspects of alliance development. Here, the relevant worksheets are noted after each segment description.

1. The Fox Cities Children's Museum and Roxanne's Doll Shoppe

A small museum in Appleton, Wisconsin, receives a large collection of dolls. With no expertise in presenting dolls and no curator on staff, its board chairman turns to local retailer, Sharon Roxanne Wallis. Wallis begins by providing volunteer service to curate the doll collection. The alliance expands to revitalization of the museum gift shop, with Wallis assuming management of the shop's ongoing operation. (Worksheets 1 and 2.)

2. City Year and Timberland

City Year operates a youth service corps that has grown from its Boston roots into a national organization sending teams of young people from diverse backgrounds into communities in need. Timberland is a successful footwear company that has branched into apparel and retail stores. The partnership starts as a contribution of boots and diversifies and grows to become strategically important to both organizations. Many benefits are exchanged. For example, Timberland provides clothing, financial support, access to helpful people, and office space for a local corps; City Year provides service opportunities and training, and makes a significant contribution to building a service culture in Timberland. (This alliance is described in more detail in James Austin's *The Collaboration Challenge*.) (Worksheets 1, 2, 6, and 7.)

3. The Stairstep Initiative and General Mills and Glory Foods

The Stairstep Initiative is a grassroots organization devoted to building up the African American community in north Minneapolis. Part of its mission is economic development through bringing jobs to an underdeveloped area of the city. Stairstep develops a vision of an inner-city manufacturing partnership that includes a Fortune 500 company, Stairstep as a community development agency, and an African American entrepreneur. General Mills agrees to partner in developing a food packaging plant. Then, by serendipity, Stairstep's founder, Alfred Babington-Johnson, discovers Glory Foods of Ohio, led by an African American entrepreneur. The resulting alliance creates Siyeza, a manufacturing plant employing sixty people from the north Minneapolis community to produce a line of family-size meals for Glory Foods. (Worksheets 6 and 7.)

4. Salvation Army Golden Diners and Bill's Restaurant

The Salvation Army Golden Diners has been serving nutritionally balanced meals to seniors for many years at community dining centers in Illinois, but the program is having problems attracting younger seniors, especially men. Seeking to expand benefits that its customers value, the Salvation Army finds Moe Procopos, owner of Bill's Restaurant, and establishes a partnership serving senior diners. The opportunity to eat at Bill's as part of the Golden Diners program increases the number of seniors served by three to five times and attracts a much more diverse clientele. (Worksheet 9.)

5. The Computer Clubhouse and Intel

The Computer Clubhouse of the Museum of Science in Boston provides an after-school learning environment for young people from underserved communities. Youths, age ten to eighteen, work with adult mentors to explore their own ideas, develop skills, and build confidence in themselves through the use of technology. By 1999, there are fifteen clubhouses in the United States and abroad and a vision of a network of Computer Clubhouses around the world. In 2000, Intel develops an alliance with the Computer Clubhouse to create at least one hundred clubhouses by 2005 in the United States and in other countries where Intel operates. By 2001, Intel is providing technology, funding, and volunteers at forty sites, along with ongoing assistance in the expansion effort. (Worksheet 11.)

Additional Resources

Drucker.org

The collaboration section of the Drucker Foundation Web site [drucker.org/collaboration/] contains the full downloadable text of this workbook, current lists of suggested readings, reference documents, suggested Web sites for research on businesses, and information about related workshops. Web site content will be updated with additional resources as they become available. Readers may subscribe to a monthly Meeting the Collaboration Challenge e-mail notice.

Alliance Roundtable

Your nonprofit may want to organize a roundtable of representatives of successful local alliances. Learning from the experience of peers, especially nonprofit leaders together with their business partners, provides a meaningful and inspiring opportunity to build understanding for meeting the collaboration challenge.

Suggested Readings

The Drucker Foundation Self-Assessment Tool

Drucker, P. F. *The Drucker Foundation Self-Assessment Tool: Participant Workbook.* San Francisco: Jossey-Bass, 1998.

Stern, G. J. *The Drucker Foundation Self-Assessment Tool: Process Guide.* San Francisco: Jossey-Bass, 1998.

Books and Articles

Andreasen, A. R. "Profits for Nonprofits: Find a Corporate Partner." *Harvard Business Review,* Nov.-Dec. 1996.

Arsenault, J. *Forging Nonprofit Alliances.* San Francisco: Jossey-Bass, 1998.

Austin, J. E. "The Invisible Side of Leadership." *Leader to Leader.* [http://drucker.org/leaderbooks/L2L/spring98/austin.html]. Spring 1998.

Austin, J. E. *The Collaboration Challenge: How Nonprofits and Businesses Succeed Through Strategic Alliances.* San Francisco: Jossey-Bass, 2000.

Dees, J. G., Emerson, J., and Economy, P. *Enterprising Nonprofits: A Toolkit for Social Entrepreneurs.* New York: Wiley, 2001.

Hesselbein, F., and Cohen, P. M. (eds.). *Leader to Leader: Enduring Insights on Leadership from the Drucker Foundation's Award-Winning Journal.* San Francisco: Jossey-Bass, 1999.

Hesselbein, F., Goldsmith, M., and Beckhard, R. (eds.). *The Leader of the Future.* San Francisco: Jossey-Bass, 1996.

Hesselbein, F., Goldsmith, M., and Beckhard, R. (eds.). *The Organization of the Future.* San Francisco: Jossey-Bass, 1997.

Hesselbein, F., Goldsmith, M., Beckhard, R., and Schubert, R. F. (eds.). *The Community of the Future.* San Francisco: Jossey-Bass, 1998.

Hesselbein, F., Goldsmith, M., and Somerville, I. (eds.). *Leading Beyond the Walls.* San Francisco: Jossey-Bass, 1999.

Hesselbein, F., Goldsmith, M., and Somerville, I. (eds.). *Leading for Innovation and Organizing for Results.* San Francisco: Jossey-Bass, 2001.

Kanter, R. M. "From Spare Change to Real Change: The Social Sector as Beta Site for Business Innovation." *Harvard Business Review,* May 1999.

Mattessich, P. W., Murray-Close, M., and Monsey, B. *Collaboration: What Makes It Work.* (2nd ed.) Minneapolis: Amherst H. Wilder Foundation, 2001.

Sagawa, S., and Segal, E. *Common Interest, Common Good: Creating Value Through Business and Social Sector Partnerships.* Boston: Harvard Business School Press, 2000.

Steckel, R., Simons, R., Lengsfelder, P., and Lehman, J. *Filthy Rich: How to Turn Your Nonprofit Fantasies into Cold, Hard Cash.* (Revised and updated.) Berkeley, Calif.: Ten Speed Press, 2000.

Stern, G. J. *Mobilize People for Marketing Success.* Minneapolis: Amherst H. Wilder Foundation, 1997.

About the Drucker Foundation

The Peter F. Drucker Foundation for Nonprofit Management, founded in 1990, takes its name and inspiration from the acknowledged father of modern management. By providing educational opportunities and resources, the foundation furthers its mission "to lead social sector organizations toward excellence in performance." It pursues this mission through the presentation of conferences, video teleconferences, the annual Peter F. Drucker Award for Nonprofit Innovation, and the annual Frances Hesselbein Community Innovation Fellows Program, as well as through the development of management resources, partnerships, and publications.

The Drucker Foundation believes that a healthy society requires three vital sectors: a public sector of effective governments, a private sector of effective businesses, and a social sector of effective community organizations. The mission of the social sector and its organizations is to change lives. It accomplishes this mission by addressing the needs of the spirit, mind, and body of individuals, the community, and society. This sector and its organizations also create a meaningful sphere of effective and responsible citizenship.

In the ten years after its inception, the Drucker Foundation, among other things:

- Presented the Drucker Innovation Award, which each year generates hundreds of applications from local community enterprises; many applicants work in fields where results are difficult to achieve.

- Worked with social sector leaders through the Frances Hesselbein Community Innovation Fellows program.

- Held more than twenty conferences in the United States and in countries around the world.

- Developed thirteen books: a *Self-Assessment Tool* (revised 1998) for nonprofit organizations; three books in the Drucker Foundation Future Series, *The Leader of the Future* (1996), *The Organization of the Future* (1997), and *The Community of the Future* (1998); *Leader to Leader* (1999); *Leading Beyond the Walls* (1999); *The Collaboration Challenge* (2000); the *Leading in a Time of Change* viewer's workbook and video (2001), *Leading for Innovation* (2002), and four Leader to Leader Guides, *On Mission and Leadership, On Leading Change, On High-Performance Organizations,* and *On Creativity, Innovation, and Renewal* (all 2002).

- Developed *Leader to Leader,* a quarterly journal for leaders from all three sectors.

- Established a Web site [drucker.org] that shares articles on leadership and management and examples of nonprofit innovation with hundreds of thousands of visitors each year.

For more information on the Drucker Foundation, contact:

The Peter F. Drucker Foundation for Nonprofit Management
320 Park Avenue, Third Floor
New York, NY 10022-6839 U.S.A.
Telephone: (212) 224-1174
Fax: (212) 224-2508
E-mail: info@pfdf.org
Web address: www.drucker.org

Customer Feedback Form

Please complete this form and return it to the Drucker Foundation. You may also complete it on-line at [drucker.org/collaboration/].

I. Tell us about your organization.

   1. Year founded. _____   2. Annual operating budget._____

   3. Area(s) in which your organization works (for example, arts, human service, education, health).

   _____

II. Tell us about your experience with the *Meeting the Collaboration Challenge Workbook.*

   4. How have you used the workbook? (Check all that apply.)

   ☐ Read the materials

   ☐ Used one or more worksheets or exercises

   ☐ Applied the ideas or concepts in my work

   5. Please respond to each of the following statements by circling the appropriate word.

   The *Meeting the Collaboration Challenge Workbook* helped us

a. Prepare our organization to meet the collaboration challenge with businesses	Yes	Somewhat	No
b. Plan strategic alliances with businesses	Yes	Somewhat	No
c. Develop alliances with businesses	Yes	Somewhat	No
d. Renew our organization's existing strategic alliances with businesses	Yes	Somewhat	No

6. Please describe any additional information, exercises, or resources you would find valuable in updated editions of this workbook or on the Drucker Foundation Web site.

III. Tell us about you.

Name/Title _____

Organization _____

Address _____

City _____ State _____ Zip _____

Telephone _____ Fax _____ E-mail _____

7. Would you like to be added to the Drucker Foundation mailing list for information on our publications, conferences, workshops, and resources?

☐ Yes   ☐ No   ☐ Already receive Drucker Foundation mailings

Please return this completed form to:

The Drucker Foundation
320 Park Avenue, 3rd Floor
New York, NY 10022-6839 USA

Telephone: (212) 224-1174

Fax: (212) 224-2508

Web site: www.drucker.org

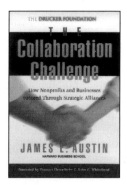

The Collaboration Challenge

How Nonprofits and Businesses Succeed Through Strategic Alliances

James E. Austin

Presented by the Drucker Foundation

In this timely and insightful book, James E. Austin provides a practical framework for understanding how traditional philanthropic relationships can be transformed into powerful strategic alliances. He offers advice and lessons drawn from the experiences of numerous collaborations, including Timberland and City Year; Starbucks and CARE; Georgia-Pacific and The Nature Conservancy; MCI WorldCom and The National Geographic Society; Reebok and Amnesty International; and Hewlett-Packard and the National Science Resource Center.

Readers will learn how to:

• Find and connect with high-potential partners

• Ensure strategic fit with a partner's mission and values

• Generate greater value for each partner and society

• Manage the partnering relationship effectively

Hardcover   ISBN 0-7879-5220-6 $25.00

Meeting the Collaboration Challenge

Peter F. Drucker Foundation for Nonprofit Management

In his book *The Collaboration Challenge*, James E. Austin of Harvard Business School demonstrated how nonprofits and businesses can work together to improve results. Now, in *Meeting the Collaboration Challenge*, the Drucker Foundation provides specific guidelines to help nonprofits of every size put collaboration into practice. This video package includes a video that chronicles five successful collaborations and a workbook that, when used with either the video or Austin's book, will help readers assess their organizations' readiness for collaboration, identify what they have to offer to private sector organizations, begin to identify organizations they might partner with, and take the first steps toward successful collaboration.

Meeting the Collaboration Challenge Video Package (includes video and workbook) ISBN 0-7879-6225-2 $55.00

Meeting the Collaboration Challenge Leader's Package (includes video, workbook, and a copy of *The Collaboration Challenge*) ISBN 0-7879-6227-9 $75.00

Meeting the Collaboration Challenge Video ISBN 0-7879-5253-8 $50.00

Meeting the Collaboration Challenge Workbook ISBN 0-7879-6231-7 $14.00

Leader to Leader Guides

Frances Hesselbein, Rob Johnston
Presented by the Drucker Foundation

Each of the four volumes in the Leader to Leader Guides—*On Mission and Leadership, On Leading Change, On High-Performance Organizations,* and *On Creativity, Innovation, and Renewal*—is organized around an essential topic with a diversity of views presented in clear, short chapters. These essential collections provide leaders with opportunities to take their organizations to new levels of excellence.

On Mission and Leadership:
A Leader to Leader Guide

ISBN: 0-7879-6068-3 $18.00

On Mission and Leadership features the best thinking of top experts on inspired leadership, vision, and mission-focused management.

On Leading Change:
A Leader to Leader Guide

ISBN: 0-7879-6070-5 $18.00

On Leading Change explores the complex challenges of shepherding organizations through change and provides leaders with strategies for change, sustaining growth, and leading transition.

On High-Performance Organizations:
A Leader to Leader Guide

ISBN: 0-7879-6069-1 $18.00

On High-Performance Organizations offers a roadmap for organizational success by revealing how leaders employ people with a diversity of experience and opinion, support efforts to anticipate and embrace change, build productive work communities, and disperse leadership responsibility.

On Creativity, Innovation, and Renewal:
A Leader to Leader Guide

ISBN: 0-7879-6067-5 $18.00

On Creativity, Innovation, and Renewal shows leaders how to establish a workplace environment that encourages creativity and innovation while creating a sense of passion and importance.

FAX
Toll Free
24 hours a day:
800-605-2665

CALL
Toll Free
6am to 5pm PST:
800-956-7739

MAIL
Jossey-Bass Publishers
989 Market St.
San Francisco, CA 94103-1741

WEB
Secure ordering at:
www.josseybass.com

Leading for Innovation

And Organizing for Results

Frances Hesselbein, Marshall Goldsmith, and Iain Somerville

From the Drucker Foundation's Wisdom to Action Series

Renowned thought leaders offer their insights on innovation

Peter Drucker defines innovation as "change that creates a new dimension of performance." Leaders can create environments, give people the tools, and set the expectation to make innovation part of daily work. In this second volume of the Drucker Foundation's Wisdom to Action Series, twenty-seven remarkable thought leaders help today's leaders meet the challenge of releasing the power of innovation.

Leading for Innovation brings together Clayton M. Christensen, Jim Collins, Howard Gardner, Charles Handy, Rosabeth Moss Kanter, C. William Pollard, Margaret Wheatley, and other thought leaders to offer practical guidance for those who seek to lead their organizations to a new dimension of performance.

These thoughtful and incisive essays are essential resources for executives from the business, nonprofit, and government sectors as well as for consultants and board members.

Hardcover   ISBN 0-7879-5359-8 $27.95

FAX	**CALL**	**MAIL**	**WEB**
Toll Free	Toll Free	Jossey-Bass Publishers	Secure ordering at:
24 hours a day:	6am to 5pm PST:	989 Market St.	www.josseybass.com
800-605-2665	800-956-7739	San Francisco, CA 94103-1741	www.leaderbooks.org

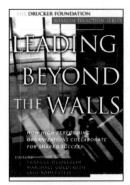

Leading Beyond the Walls

Frances Hesselbein, Marshall Goldsmith,
Iain Somerville, Editors

from the Drucker Foundation's Wisdom to Action Series

"There is need for acceptance on the part of leaders in every single institution, and in every single sector, that they, as leaders, have two responsibilities. They are responsible and accountable for the performance of their institution, and that has to be concentrated, focused, limited. They are responsible however, also, for the community as a whole. This requires commitment. It requires willingness to accept that other institutions have different values, respect for these values, and willingness to learn what these values are. It requires hard work. But above all, it requires commitment; conviction; dedication to the Common Good. Yes, each institution is autonomous and has to do its own work the way each instrument in an orchestra plays its own part. But there is also the 'score,' the community. And only if the individual instrument contributes to the score is there music. Otherwise there is only noise. This book is about the score."
—Peter F. Drucker

Increasingly, leaders and their organizations work in ways that extend beyond the walls of the enterprise. These partnerships, alliances, and networks allow organizations to achieve new levels of performance. At the same time, they create new challenges. Leaders "beyond the walls" must be adept at building and maintaining relationships, comfortable in working with individuals and organizations they cannot control, and able to move beyond the old preconceptions.

Leading Beyond the Walls presents insights from over twenty-five thought leaders from all three sectors, exploring the challenges and opportunities of partnership as well as the unique practices and perspectives that have helped individuals and organizations become more effective.

Paperback ISBN 0-7879-5555-8 $16.50

FAX	CALL	MAIL	WEB
Toll Free	Toll Free	Jossey-Bass Publishers	Secure ordering at:
24 hours a day:	6am to 5pm PST:	989 Market St.	www.josseybass.com
800-605-2665	800-956-7739	San Francisco, CA 94103-1741	

Leading in a Time of Change

A conversation between Peter F. Drucker and
Peter M. Senge

Peter F. Drucker, Peter M. Senge, and Frances Hesselbein

Sit at the table with the visionary leaders who are setting
the agenda for organizational leadership and change.

The Drucker Foundation presents a conversation
with Peter F. Drucker and Peter M. Senge, hosted by
Frances Hesselbein. In this dynamic package—which
includes a video and companion workbook—two
great minds of modern management share their
wisdom on how leaders can prepare themselves and
their organizations for the inevitable changes that lie
ahead.

Watch the video and witness a remarkable conversation between Peter Drucker
and Peter Senge as they talk about the importance of learning to lead change for
all organizations. Using the principles presented in this stimulating video and workbook, you can help transform your organization into a change leader. In their discussion Drucker and Senge reveal how you can:

• Develop systematic methods to look for and anticipate change.

• Focus on and invest in opportunities rather than problems.

• Phase out established products and services.

• Balance change and continuity.

• Motivate and retain top performers and create a mind-set among employees that
  embraces positive change.

The companion workbook will be an invaluable aid in making strategic decisions.
It will also serve as a fundamental resource for planning and implementing changes
within your organization. This extraordinary package is an ideal tool for executive
retreats, management training, and personal leadership development.

42-minute video with companion Viewer's Workbook ISBN 0-7879-5603-1 $195.00

FAX	CALL	MAIL	WEB
Toll Free	Toll Free	Jossey-Bass Publishers	Secure ordering at:
24 hours a day:	6am to 5pm PST:	989 Market St.	www.josseybass.com
800-605-2665	800-956-7739	San Francisco, CA 94103-1741	

Lessons in Leadership

Peter F. Drucker

Over the span of his sixty-year career, Peter F. Drucker has worked with many exemplary leaders in the non-profit sector, government, and business. In the course of his work, he has observed these leaders closely and learned from them the attributes of effective leadership. In this video, Drucker presents inspirational portraits of five outstanding leaders, showing how each brought different strengths to the task, and shares the lessons we can learn from their approaches to leadership. Drucker's insights (plus the accompanying *Facilitator's Guide* and *Workbook*) will help participants identify which methods work best for them and how to recognize their own particular strengths in leadership.

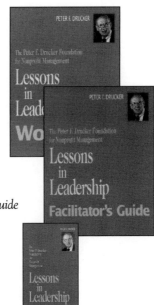

1 20-minute video + 1 *Facilitator's Guide* + 1 *Workbook*
ISBN 0-7879-4497-1 $95.00

Excellence in Nonprofit Leadership

Peter F. Drucker, Max De Pree, Frances Hesselbein

This video package is a powerful three-in-one development program for building more effective nonprofit organizations and boards. *Excellence in Nonprofit Leadership* presents three modules that can be used independently or sequentially to help nonprofit boards and staff strengthen leadership throughout the organization. The video contains three twenty-minute programs: (I) *Lessons in Leadership* with Peter Drucker (as described above); (II) *Identifying the Needs of Followers*, with Max De Pree and Michele Hunt; and (III) *Leading Through Mission*, with Frances Hesselbein. The video comes with one *Facilitator's Guide*, which contains complete instructions for leading all three programs, and one free *Workbook*, which is designed to help participants deepen and enrich the learning experience.

1 60-minute video + 1 *Facilitator's Guide* + 1 *Workbook*
ISBN 0-7879-4496-3 $140.00

FAX
Toll Free
24 hours a day:
800-605-2665

CALL
Toll Free
6am to 5pm PST:
800-956-7739

MAIL
Jossey-Bass Publishers
989 Market St.
San Francisco, CA 94103-1741

WEB
Secure ordering at:
www.josseybass.com

The Drucker Foundation Self-Assessment Tool

Since its original publication in 1993, the best-selling *Drucker Foundation Self-Assessment Tool* has helped and inspired countless nonprofit boards, executives, and teams to rediscover the direction and potential of their organizations. This completely revised edition of the *Self-Assessment Tool* now offers even more powerful guidance to help organizations uncover the truth about their performance, focus their direction, and take control of their future.

The *Self-Assessment Tool* combines long-range planning and strategic marketing with a passion for dispersed leadership. It allows an organization to plan for results, to learn from its customers, and to release the energy of its people to further its mission. The *Process Guide* by Gary J. Stern provides step-by-step guidelines and self-assessment resources, while the *Participant Workbook* by Peter F. Drucker features thoughtful introductions and clear worksheets. Participants will not only gain new insights about their organization's potential, but also forge strategies for implementation and future success.

Multiple Uses for the *Self-Assessment Tool*

- *The leadership team*—the chairman of the board and the chief executive—can lead the organization in conducting a comprehensive self-assessment, refining mission, goals, and results, and developing a working plan of action.

- *Teams throughout the organization* can use the *Tool* to invigorate projects, tailoring the process to focus on specific areas as needed.

- *Governing boards* can use the *Tool* in orientation for new members, as means to deepen thinking during retreats, and to develop clarity on mission and goals.

- *Working groups from collaborating organizations* can use the *Tool* to define common purpose and to develop clear goals, programs, and plans.

Process Guide   Paperback ISBN 0-7879-4436-X $30.00
Participant Workbook   Paperback ISBN 0-7879-4437-8 $14.00

1+1 SAT Package = 1 *Process Guide* + 1 *Participant Workbook*
ISBN 0-7879-4730-X $35.00 **Save 20%!**

1+10 SAT Package = 1 *Process Guide* + 10 *Participant Workbooks*
ISBN 0-7879-4731-8 $95.00 **Save 40%!**

FAX	CALL	MAIL	WEB
Toll Free	Toll Free	Jossey-Bass Publishers	Secure ordering at:
24 hours a day:	6am to 5pm PST:	989 Market St.	www.josseybass.com
800-605-2665	800-956-7739	San Francisco, CA 94103-1741	

Leader to Leader

A quarterly publication of the
Drucker Foundation and
Jossey-Bass Publishers

Frances Hesselbein, Editor-in-Chief

Leader to Leader is a unique management publication, a quarterly report on management, leadership, and strategy written by today's top leaders *themselves*. Four times a year, *Leader to Leader* keeps you ahead of the curve by bringing you the latest offerings from a peerless selection of world-class executives, best-selling management authors, leading consultants, and respected social thinkers, making *Leader to Leader* unlike any other magazine or professional publication today.

Think of it as a short, intensive seminar with today's top thinkers and doers—people like Peter F. Drucker, Rosabeth Moss Kanter, Max De Pree, Charles Handy, Esther Dyson, Stephen Covey, Meg Wheatley, Peter Senge, and others.

Subscriptions to **Leader to Leader** are $199.00.
501(c)(3) nonprofit organizations can subscribe for $99.00 (must supply tax-exempt ID number when subscribing). Prices subject to change without notice.

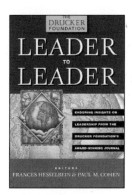

Leader to Leader

Enduring Insights on Leadership from the
Drucker Foundation's Award-Winning Journal
Frances Hesselbein, Paul M. Cohen, Editors

The world's thought leaders come together in *Leader to Leader*, an inspiring examination of mission, leadership, values, innovation, building collaborations, shaping effective institutions, and creating community. Management pioneer Peter F. Drucker; Southwest Airlines CEO Herb Kelleher; best-selling authors Warren Bennis, Stephen R. Covey, and Charles Handy; Pulitzer Prize winner Doris Kearns Goodwin; Harvard professors Rosabeth Moss Kanter and Regina Herzlinger; and learning organization expert Peter Senge are among those who share their knowledge and experience in this essential resource. Their essays will spark ideas, open doors, and inspire all those who face the challenge of leading in an ever-changing environment.

For a reader's guide, see www.leaderbooks.org

Hardcover   ISBN 0-7879-4726-1 $27.00

FAX	**CALL**	**MAIL**	**WEB**
Toll Free	Toll Free	Jossey-Bass Publishers	Secure ordering at:
24 hours a day:	6am to 5pm PST:	989 Market St.	www.josseybass.com
800-605-2665	800-956-7739	San Francisco, CA 94103-1741	